To Mrs. Anderson
With Love
Ashley Hoskins 1996

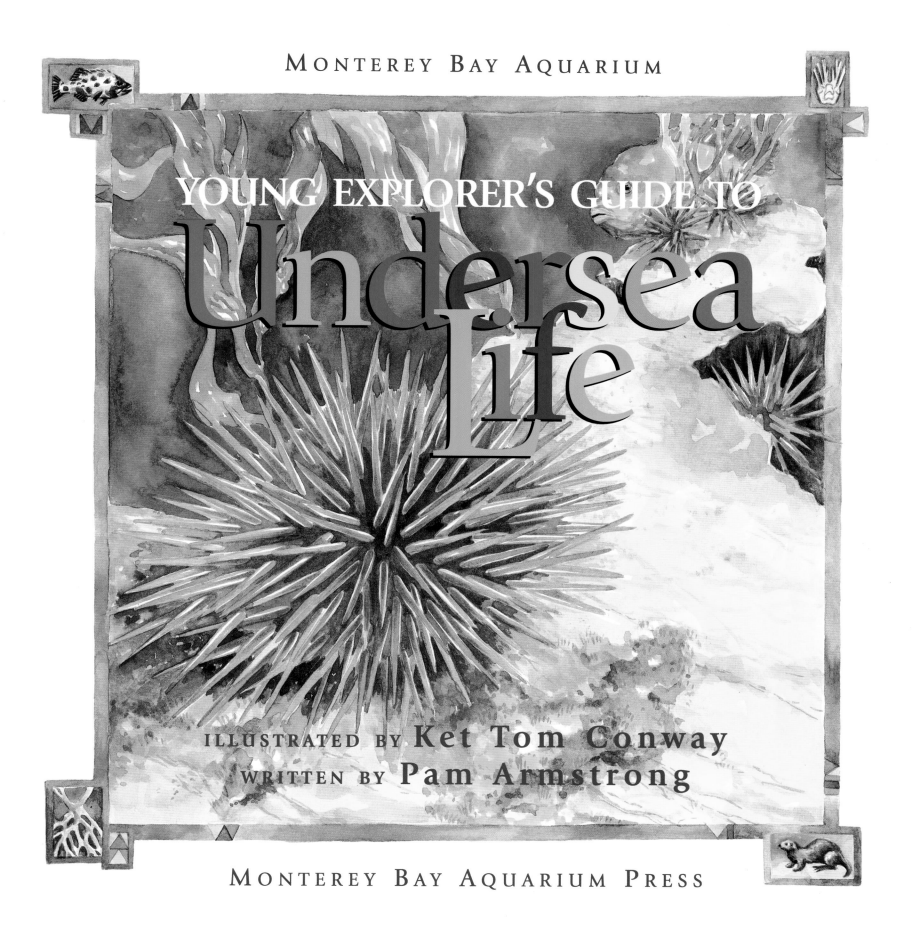

MONTEREY BAY AQUARIUM

YOUNG EXPLORER'S GUIDE TO
Undersea Life

ILLUSTRATED BY Ket Tom Conway
WRITTEN BY Pam Armstrong

MONTEREY BAY AQUARIUM PRESS

To my brother, Steve, who began my awe for the sea, and to my husband, Mike, who continually renews it. —Ket

For my son, Mike, who always asks me why. —Pam

Monterey Bay Aquarium Foundation
886 Cannery Row
Monterey, California 93940

Design: Ann W. Douden
Managing Editor: Nora L. Deans
Project Editor: Lisa M. Tooker

Library of Congress Catalog Card Number:96-1051
ISBN: 1-878244-10-8
Printed in Hong Kong through Global Interprint
Distributed to the book trade by Publishers Group West

Pssst . . . over here! It's time to go exploring! You'll need your special explorer's clothes—the ones that can go under water. Are you ready? We're taking a storybook trip to the sea. You'll discover tiny, tiny plants and animals that drift through the ocean. And seaweeds that decorate rocks. There are creatures that don't have backbones. And fishes of all shapes and sizes. You'll discover birds that dive into the water to catch their food. And meet mammals, like you, that come to the water's surface to breathe. Now, turn the page, *come closer and discover the wonders of the sea.*

Plankton

Plankton are plants and animals that drift through the ocean. There are trillions and trillions of them in the sea. Most plankton are so small a hundred could fit on the tip of your finger. And so many grow that sometimes huge swarms of plant plankton cloud the water. But before long, hungry animal plankton drifting by gobble up the plant plankton. Then anchovies, other fishes and jellies find both plant and animal plankton and gobble them up, too. Plankton are some of the most important animals and plants in the sea because so many other animals eat them.

Plankton

Gardens of lacy, green sea lettuce decorate rocks along the seashore. At high tide, sea lettuce lives under water. But when the tide goes out, this seaweed must survive the hot, drying sun. Sea lettuce grows like a weed, covering large areas and crowding out other plants. Many animals eat this plant. A hungry turban snail creeps up and nibbles on its blades. Then a shore crab crawls by and does the same thing. For snails and crabs, sea lettuce makes a delicious salad. But for you and me, lettuce that comes from farms and backyard gardens is the most pleasing.

Ulva spp.

A giant kelp plant sways with the ocean's waves. This brown seaweed grows tall to the water's surface where it collects sunlight for energy to grow. The long stipe is like a plant's stem, strong and bendable. At its bottom, a strong base anchors the plant to the rocky seafloor, keeping it from tearing loose and floating away. Many kelp plants grow close to each other. Together they create an underwater forest that's home to sea urchins, crabs, snails, sea otters and many other creatures.

Flashing brilliant rainbow colors, a purple sea slug slowly crawls across the rocky seafloor. Soft, bright orange spines on its back gently wave with the water's currents. A sea slug is so colorful, it may be the most beautiful slug you've ever seen. But it has a surprise for other animals. It tastes terrible to nearly anything that eats it. And once a fish or other sea creature has a taste, this slug's bright colors may be a reminder: "Beware! I taste terrible. Don't eat me!"

Flabellinopsis iodinea

A sea star creeps ever so slowly across a tide pool. Thousands of special tube feet hidden under her body work together to help her move. When a wave crashes on the rock, the sea star is ready. Powerful suction cups at the tip of each tube foot hold tightly to the rock, keeping the sea star from washing out to sea. Once the wave is gone, the sea star moves on until she finds a tasty mussel glued to a rock. Settling her body over the mussel, she slowly pulls its shells apart with the power of her tube feet. Then she eats the mussel's soft body inside.

Pisaster ochraceus

A purple shore crab marches down the rocks to a nearby tide pool. Suddenly, a wave comes in close and he scurries sideways back to his little crack in the rocks. Squeezing into a tight spot, the crab holds on with his legs until the wave has washed back out. When the coast is clear, the crab slowly inches his way out and heads back down the rocky slope. Along the way, he stops in a seaweed garden. Using his large claws, he harvests a tasty salad of small green algae growing on the rocks.

Hemigrapsus nudus

A by-the-wind sailor floats on the surface of the water, usually far out to sea. With tentacles that dangle from her body, she catches and eats tiny plankton as they pass by. When a strong wind blows, she's carried with thousands of other by-the-wind sailors up onto the beach. The angle of her sail determines where she'll land. If her sail points one way, she'll end up on the west coast of the United States. If it angles the other way, she'll sail to Japan. What if you could only go where the wind blows? Which way would you angle your sail?

PACIFIC OCEAN

Velella velella

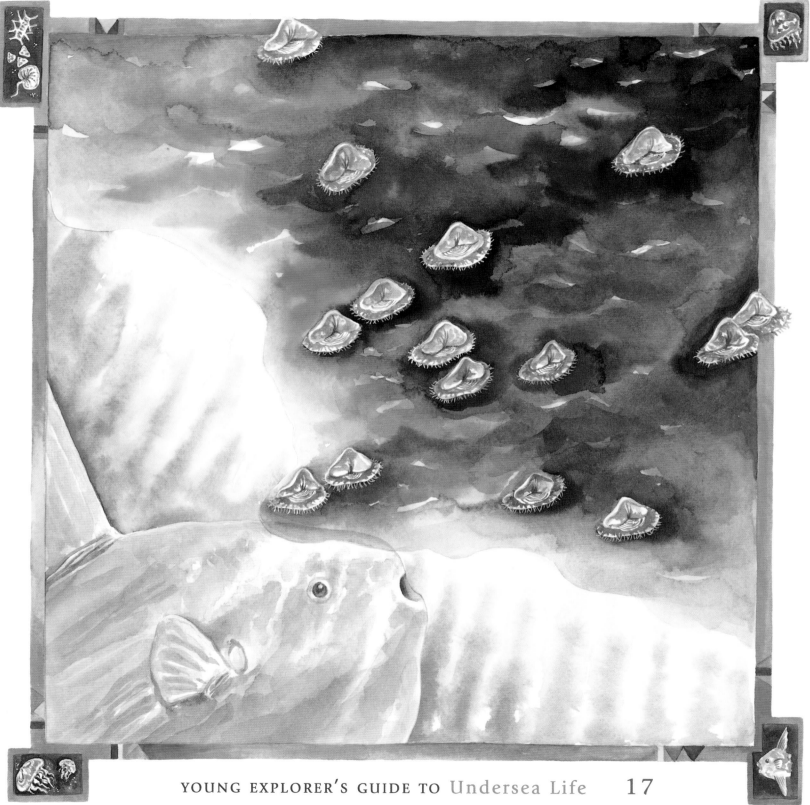

A moon jelly gently pulses her body . . . open, closed, open, closed . . . as she moves through the water. She rides the currents of the sea the way a leaf rides the winds on land. The currents carry her along with other drifting animals. All of a sudden, a sea turtle swims up. With nowhere to hide in the wide open sea, the moon jelly gets eaten by the hungry turtle. But there are hundreds and hundreds of other moon jellies in the sea. Some stay at sea. Others drift up on beaches where they look like gooey blobs of jelly.

Aurelia aurita

Shy and curious, a giant Pacific octopus hides in the rocks all day. At night, he slips out of his home and explores the rocky seafloor. His eight long arms reach and poke into rocky cracks as he searches for crabs, scallops and other small animals to eat. Spying a crab, the octopus swiftly covers the meal with his body. He holds the crab tightly with strong arms. Powerful suction cups on the underside of each arm help hold the wriggling meal. Then the octopus cracks open the crab's shell with a strong beak that's hidden in his mouth.

Octopus dofleini

Thousands of milky white squid swim together in a huge school. Sometimes they dart with quick bursts of speed. Other times they slowly cruise along in search of food. Spying a school of small fishes, they swim right into the middle of it. Each squid grabs for a meal by snapping one of its longest tentacles like a whip. Suddenly, a hungry blue shark swims up. The school of squid scatters this way and that, and many of them release squirts of dark ink stored in a sac inside each one's body. The ink confuses the shark, and the squid zip away.

Loligo opalescens

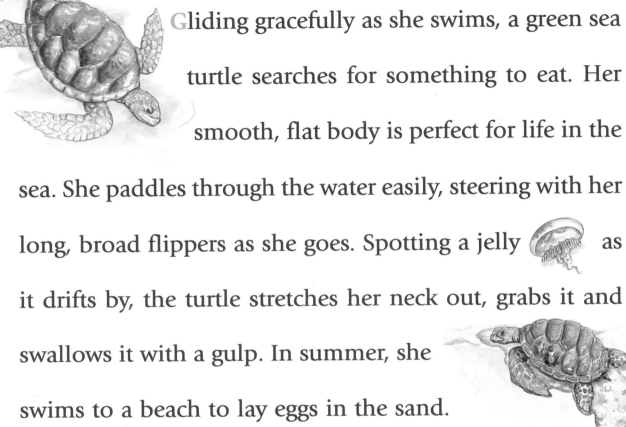

Gliding gracefully as she swims, a green sea turtle searches for something to eat. Her smooth, flat body is perfect for life in the sea. She paddles through the water easily, steering with her long, broad flippers as she goes. Spotting a jelly as it drifts by, the turtle stretches her neck out, grabs it and swallows it with a gulp. In summer, she swims to a beach to lay eggs in the sand. Then she returns to sea, leaving them to hatch on their own. The baby turtles scramble across the beach and swim away.

Chelonia mydas

A quillback rockfish hunts for small fishes to eat. His speckled body blends in with the colors of the rocks, helping him hide from other animals. Spotting a small fish to eat, the quillback opens his large mouth and sucks in his meal. Suddenly, a lingcod appears, and the rockfish readies his spiny quills, sticking them up from the fin on his back. If you were a lingcod, these spines would warn you: "Stay away, or else you'll get a prickly meal!"

Sebastes maliger

Wolf eel

A wolf eel hides in cracks in the rocks. Her long, slender body curves and bends to fit snugly in her narrow, winding home. Waiting patiently, she watches for a snail or other small animal to wander too close. When one does, the wolf eel grabs the meal and holds it with strong, pointed teeth in front of her mouth. Flat teeth in the back (like the flat teeth in the back of your mouth) crush the hard shells. After she swallows her meal, she settles back in and waits, watching for another small animal to wander by.

Anarrhichthys ocellatus

An ocean sunfish lazily flaps his long fins as he cruises at the sea's surface. His stumpy tail steers as he goes. Hungry for a meal, the sunfish paddles more quickly, grabbing jellies and other soft animals as they drift by. Living in a world with no rocks to hide behind, a sunfish's light and dark coloring helps him blend in with the waters around him. When you look up at him, his light belly blends in with sunlight streaming down from above. Looking down, it's hard to see the sunfish's dark back against the darkness below.

Mola mola

Flashing silver with every turn, thousands of schooling anchovies dart through the water. They swim within inches of one another without bumping. Imagine swimming this way, quickly sensing and following each other's every move. Then you open your mouth wide and collect tiny plankton to eat as the water rushes in. But you better keep moving, or you could become a meal for an even bigger fish, or a seabird or a sea lion.

A yellowfin tuna swims thousands of miles across the world's oceans. The special shape of her body and tail helps her swim these great distances. She travels in huge schools with other yellowfin tuna. If a bigger fish or killer whale tries to eat her, or if she sees a tasty meal, she takes off in a quick burst of speed. Other times, she tucks her fins into shallow pockets on the sides of her body and glides through the water.

Thunnus albacares

A leopard shark prowls for something to eat. As he moves, his bold spots and stripes blend in with the seafloor below.

A larger shark swims by, but is fooled and swims right past the hidden leopard shark. The leopard shark won't miss his meal though.

Using his keen sense of smell, the shark searches for fishes, crabs, shrimp and other small animals to eat. Suddenly, he knows there's a fish nearby. Feeling and following the fish's movements, he chases and catches it. Then, with a quick gulp, the shark eats his meal.

Triakis semifasciata

Each spring, an Arctic tern flies all the way from the South Pole to the North Pole. Along the way, she stops to eat. Darting this way and that, she twists and turns in the air, searching for small fishes to eat. Then with a splash, she dives into the water and snatches her meal. After weeks of flying and eating, she finally arrives in the North Pole.

There she lays three eggs and spends the summer raising her young. Come fall, she returns once again to warmer weather at the South Pole.

Sterna paradisaea

A hungry brown pelican flies high overhead. Spotting something to eat in the sea below, he tucks in his wings and dives into the ocean with a big splash. He opens his large pouch and scoops up a mouthful of anchovies and shrimp to eat, then pops back up to the surface. A hook at the tip of his upper beak helps hold the slippery fish inside his pouch. The pelican dips his beak down to drain out the water. Then he tips his head back and swallows the fish whole.

Each year, a common loon travels back and forth between her two homes. In winter, she lives at sea. But in spring, she flies many miles to her summer home, a freshwater lake in the north. Hearing a mournful cry from across the lake, she follows the sound to her mate. Together, they build a nest of sticks at the lake's edge and guard their two eggs. When the young hatch, they quickly learn to swim and catch their own meals. Sometimes a young loon climbs onto a parent's back and gets a ride!

Gavia immer

A double-crested cormorant swims under the water, chasing small fishes to eat. Missing her meal, she returns to the surface and waits. Then she dives down again, paddling hard with her large, webbed feet, and catches a slippery fish. The cormorant has special feathers that keep her from floating back to the surface. This helps her swim under water. But this also means her feathers get very, very wet. Sitting on a rock after her dive, she holds out her wings and "hangs" them to dry in the sun.

A playful sea otter frolics in the ocean. Her sleek body tumbles and rolls as she goes. Hungry for a meal, she dives down to the rocky seafloor in search of sea stars, crabs, abalone or other small animals to eat. Using her strong front paws, she picks a sea urchin from the seafloor and tucks a small rock in a pocket of skin under her arm. Back at the surface, she lies on her back and sets the rock on her chest. Smashing the urchin against the rock, she cracks open the hard shell and eats the tasty meal.

Enhydra lutris

Standing tall, a male northern elephant seal rears back his head, flings up his long snout and bellows a loud snort. Other males hear the warning: "Stay away! This is my area!" All around the big male elephant seal sprawl hundreds of other female elephant seals. They came to shore to have their babies. While they're on land, the adults don't eat. But the young pups do. They drink their mothers' rich milk. By spring, the hungry adults return to the sea where they feast on squid, octopus and fishes that live in deep water.

Mirounga angustirostris

A California sea lion gracefully glides through the water. Gently twisting and turning, she paddles with her large, front flippers and steers with her flippers in back. Sometimes, she swims quite fast, leaping from the water and diving back down. Other times she dives down deep to hunt for squid, fishes and other animals to eat. Finished with her meal, she climbs up on a rock. On her front flippers, she scoots and drags her body along until she finds a place to rest.

Zalophus californianus

With great leaps and splashes, a bottlenose dolphin playfully swims in the sea. Sometimes he surfs the waves, riding them close to shore. Other times he frolics in the wake behind a boat. After playing and playing and then playing some more, the dolphin gets hungry. He chases squid or fishes through the water, then catches and holds them with teeth shaped like cones. But a dolphin is a mammal, just like you and me. Soon he must return to the surface to breathe air. Then he dives back down for more food and play.

Tursiops truncatus

A gray whale is one of the biggest animals on Earth, almost as big as a school bus. But for her enormous size, she eats tiny, tiny animals that live in the mud. Swimming on her side along the ocean floor, she scoops up a giant mouthful of mud. Then she squishes the mud out through the baleen that hangs from the top of her mouth in place of teeth. The baleen works like a giant comb, letting the mud ooze through, but trapping thousands of tiny animals on the inside. Then she licks off the animals with her gigantic tongue and swallows them.

Eschrichtius robustus

HAWAIIAN
ISLANDS

A male humpback whale sings beautiful songs under water. To us, these songs sound like whistles and moans, crackles and chirps. He sings most of his songs near Hawaii where he lives during the winter. His songs may warn other males to stay away. Or maybe females hear the songs and swim near him.

As he sings, he slowly changes the sounds, creating new songs every year. Come spring, the humpback returns to the cold waters off Alaska where he eats squid, small fishes, krill and other animals that live in the sea.

ALASKA

Megaptera novaeangliae

A killer whale is well-named, for he is one of the best hunters in the sea. Sometimes he races through the ocean, chasing large fishes to eat. His powerful tail helps him swim with tremendous speed. Then he leaps from the water and splashes back down—kersplash! Other times he snatches a seabird, resting at the sea's surface. Other killer whales work together in groups. They attack and eat seals and parts of whales that are even larger than themselves.

Orcinus orca

The Monterey Bay Aquarium is a non-profit, public institution. One goal lies behind all we do: to help protect the world's oceans.

Congratulations! Now you're an explorer!

And now you know more about the plants and animals that live in the sea. But keep exploring—there's so much more to discover! And remember . . . if we all take care of the Earth, and respect all the plants and animals that live here, they'll have lots of safe places to live. And we'll have lots of wonderful places to explore.

Glossary

adaptation: a body part, body shape, behavior or other characteristic that helps a plant or animal live in its home

algae (singular—alga): simple plants that don't have seeds; for instance, seaweeds

animal: a living thing that must find and eat its own food; for instance, a bird, fish, snail or person

baleen: tough, flexible bristles in the mouths of baleen whales that are used to strain small fishes and other prey out of the water or mud

bird: a warm-blooded animal with feathers that lays eggs

blade: the leaflike part of a seaweed

blow: a whale's spout, or exhaled breath, at the surface of the water

blowhole: a breathing nostril on top of a whale's head

camouflage: a behavior, shape, color and/or pattern that helps a plant or animal hide from its predators or prey

cold-blooded: an animal whose body temperature changes to match the outside temperature; for instance, a turtle, snake or fish

conservation: the practice of protecting nature from loss or damage

current: moving water

fish: a cold-blooded animal with fins, scales and gills

food chain: a sequence of plants and animals that shows who eats whom; the direction food energy is transferred from one creature to the next, like from the kelp plant to a sea urchin to a sea otter

Glossary

gill: a body part that helps with breathing; an organ where blood vessels absorb oxygen from the water and release carbon dioxide into the water

habitat: the place where a plant or animal lives (its home)

holdfast: the part of a seaweed that attaches it to the seafloor

invertebrate: an animal without a backbone

kelp: any of the large brown seaweeds; for instance, giant kelp (*Macrocystis*)

Macrocystis: the scientific name of giant kelp

mammal: a warm-blooded animal with hair that breathes air and nurses its live-born young

migration: an animal's seasonal travels from one region to another (like the gray whale's journey between feeding and breeding areas)

ocean: the body of salt water that covers three-quarters of the Earth's surface

phytoplankton: plant plankton

plankton: plants and animals (mostly tiny, but some large, like jellies) that drift with ocean currents

plant: a living thing that gets its energy to grow from sunlight

pollution: harmful things that make a place unsafe for plants and animals to live

predator: an animal that kills and eats other animals

Glossary

prey: an animal that is killed and eaten by a predator

reptile: a cold-blooded animal with scales that breathes air with lungs and usually lays eggs; for instance, a turtle, dinosaur, lizard, crocodile or snake

schooling: several to hundreds of fishes swimming together in a very coordinated manner

sea: the body of salt water that covers three-quarters of the Earth's surface

seafloor: the bottom of the ocean

seaweed: algae and other plants that live in the sea

spout: a whale's blow, or exhaled breath, at the surface of the water

stipe: the stemlike part of a kelp plant

tentacle: a bendable arm, either long or short, that an animal uses to catch food or protect itself

tide: the daily rise and fall of the sea along a shore

tide pool: a pool of water left along the shore as the tide level falls

tube foot: one of many little feet that look like tubes; used for moving, like a sea star crawling across rocks

vertebrate: an animal with a backbone

warm-blooded: an animal that keeps a constant body temperature regardless of the outside temperature; for instance, a bird or mammal

zooplankton: animal plankton